Carnivals Around The

Written by Christine Butterworth

Contents

London

Carnival in England

We love carnival in England.

We have a big street party every summer.

2

We sing and we dance
to the music.

New
Orleans

Carnival in North America

We love carnival in North America.

We have a big street party every spring.

We march in the street.
We wear beads.

Rio de Janeiro

Carnival in South America

We love carnival in South America.

We have a big street party every summer.

We dance to the music
all day and
all night.

7

Carnival in Greece

Rethimnon

We love carnival in Greece.

We have a big street party every spring.

We wear costumes and
we dance down the street.

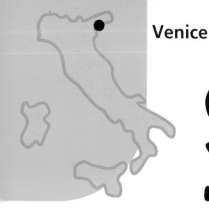
Venice

Carnival in Italy

We love carnival in Italy.

We have a big street party every winter.

10

We all wear masks.

We wear special carnival costumes.

Carnivals Around The World